A Day With A
Chumash

A Day With A
Chumash

by Georgia Lee

Illustrations by Giorgio Bacchin

RP

Runestone Press/Minneapolis

A Division of the Lerner Publishing Group

Thanks to Dr. John Johnson of the Santa Barbara
Museum of National History for editorial
comments and to Silvia Vassena of Jaca Book for
her enthusiastic assistance.

All words that appear in **bold** are explained in the
glossary that starts on page 43.

This edition first published in the United States in 1999 by Runestone Press.

Copyright © 1998 Editoriale Jaca Book SpA, Milano. All rights reserved.
Originally produced in 1998 by Editoriale Jaca Book, Milan, Italy.

Runestone Press, c/o The Lerner Publishing Group
241 First Avenue North, Minneapolis, MN 55401 U.S.A.

Captions translated by Dominique Clift.

Library of Congress Cataloging-in-Publication Data

Lee, Georgia, 1926–
A day with a Chumash / by Georgia Lee ; illustrations by Giorgio Bacchin.
        p.   cm. — (A day with—)
                    Includes index.
Summary: Presents both factual information and a fictional story on the
customs and daily life of the Chumash, an ancient civilization that
lived along the California coast 9,000 years ago.
            ISBN 0-8225-1918-6 (lib. bdg. : alk. paper)
    1. Chumash Indians—Social life and customs—Juvenile literature.
    [1. Chumash Indians. 2. Indians of North America—California.]
            I. Bacchin, Giorgio, ill. II. Title. III. Series.
                    E99.C815L44   1999
            305.898—dc21   98-35161

Manufactured in the United States of America
        1 2 3 4 5 6 – JR – 04 03 02 01 00 99

CONTENTS

INTRODUCTION

The ancestors of Native Americans, also called American Indians, inhabited North America before Europeans arrived in the 1500s. North America ranges from tropical (hot and lush) to arctic (cold and snowy) in climate. Bounded by oceans to the east and west, the continent is crossed by wild rivers and lined with jutting mountain ranges. Plains stretch across North America, and huge lakes dot its surface. Deserts and woodlands spread over many regions.

Early Native American cultures adapted to the environments in which they lived. In coastal regions, Native Americans hunted sea creatures and collected shellfish from the ocean waters. Inland river and lake Indians netted or speared freshwater fish in creeks, lakes, and rivers. On the wide, grassy plains, Native Americans hunted buffalo by throwing spears, by shooting arrows, or by luring the animals over cliffs. In the forests, some folks hunted deer and small mammals. In other parts of the continent, farmers grew corn, beans, and squash in small plots or large fields. Houses and clothing varied, too.

Native American belief systems also reflected environments. Some religions revolved around animals and successful hunting, the weather, the changing seasons, or the ocean. Many belief systems were **animist,** which gave every object a spirit.

Over centuries, Native Americans traveled from one end of the continent to the other and sometimes back again. These movements are remembered in the oral histories of many Indian nations and can be traced in the groups of languages that people speak. Ancient American Indians spoke more than 200 distinct languages, with thousands of dialects.

Some North American civilizations grew into huge empires ruled by powerful leaders. Large populations flooded cities that were later deserted. Small towns and villages flourished, as did nomadic communities. No one was rich or poor in some cultures, but in others some members lived in splendor while their neighbors shivered in small dwellings.

Trade routes linked people across the continent, bringing goods and new ideas from faraway places. The idea of pottery traveled from modern-day Mexico to what would later become the southwestern United States. Other people may have traded buffalo hides or meat for farm produce.

The ancient Chumash lived along the coast of what would become California. They developed strong trade ties with other Native American groups in the area. This story, set about 500 years ago, tells about a Chumash family near the present-day city of Santa Barbara.

Series Editors

PART ONE

THE WORLD OF THE CHUMASH

Between 15,000 and 20,000 Native Americans known as the Chumash once lived in villages built along the coast of what would become California. At least 9,000 years ago, the Chumash first tucked their villages into bluffs and near sandy coves along the Pacific Ocean, particularly in the area between present-day Santa Barbara and Malibu. Chumash territory also extended northward to a point near San Simeon and then inland and southward to the Mount Piños area. The Chumash settled on what came to be known as the Channel Islands—Santa Cruz, Santa Rosa, and San Miguel—located just off the coast of present-day Santa Barbara. The Chumash spoke several related languages.

The Chumash, like most Native American groups in California, were hunter-gatherers who obtained food by hunting animals, fishing, and gathering wild nuts, berries, and plants. To maintain this way of life, some Native American groups moved from one place to the next after they had exhausted nearby resources. Chumash life was different, however. In an average year, wild food plants grew abundantly in the mild climate. Game animals and seafood were plentiful. Usually the villages had freshwater streams nearby.

(Above) *In this scene from a California Native American settlement, hunters try to kill a whale beached at low tide. Whales were a valuable source of food, blubber, and bones.* (Left) *This tranquil bay is typical of those found in Chumash territory.*

Such favorable conditions allowed the Chumash to settle in coastal towns. Villagers made occasional trips inland to gather important foods, such as **piñon** (pine) nuts, **chia** seeds, and acorns. The Chumash ground acorns into a coarse powder, which they shaped into cakes and let harden for easy storage. To prepare acorn mush or soup, Chumash women added water to the cakes and heated them. The Chumash packed the highly nutritious chia seeds from the sage plant for long trips.

(Right) *This map of the North American continent shows present-day California and Baja California, a part of Mexico, in brown. The purple area is the great basin, an elevated region bounded by the Wasatch Mountains and the Sierra Nevada. (Below) This map defines the boundaries of the original Chumash territory in southern California. The place names used in modern times are those applied later by the Spaniards.*

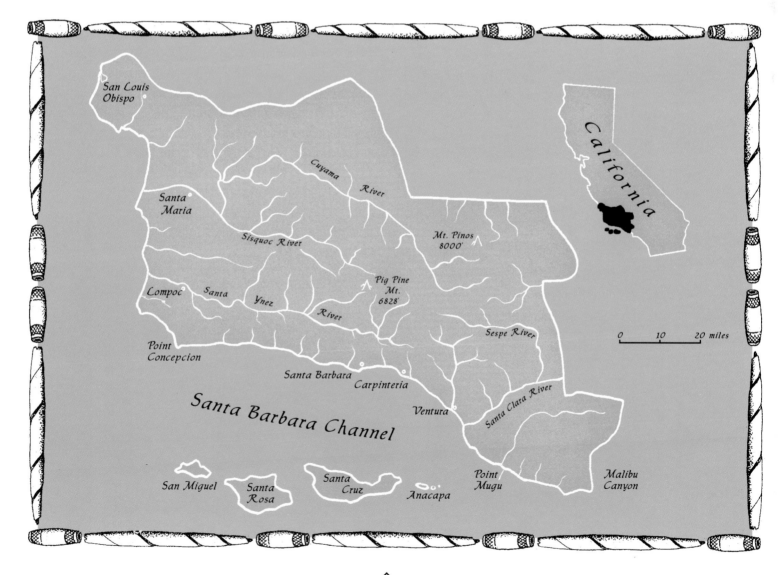

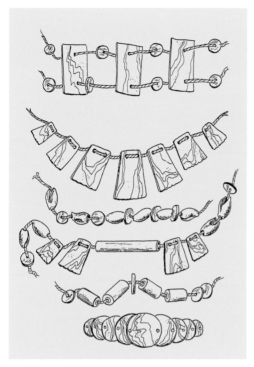

(Above left) *The Chumash used shells to make jewelry. They pierced some shells and strung them together. Other shells were engraved, painted, and mounted on leather strips to create elaborate designs. The Chumash wore jewelry for special occasions or to indicate their social status.* (Above right) *The Chumash used a mortar (the bowl) and pestle (the grinding instrument) to mash stones into a fine dust to make pigments. To the right of the mortar is an abalone shell, which the Chumash used as a bowl.* (Left) *When Native American hunters killed an animal, they were careful to use every part of it. Shells and animal bones became tools or charms. The ceremonial dagger was carved from the femur of a grizzly bear.* (Below, left) *Modern-day Chumash paddle an oceangoing sewn plank canoe.* (Below, right) *The Chumash expressed their strong ties to the sea through their artwork and ceremonies. This* **rock painting** *from Pletto Creek represents a dancer in the guise of a swordfish.*

The Chumash also acquired food and resources through trade. **Tomols,** oceangoing canoes, were used for fishing and for traveling back and forth between the mainland and the islands. The Chumash traded **shell beads** for **obsidian** with the Yokuts who lived to the east. Gabrielino traders from the south brought **soapstone** bowls.

Because food was easy to obtain, the Chumash had time to become highly skilled artisans. Craftspeople carved shell beads that they made into ornaments and necklaces. Others worked wood into bowls. Finely carved stone bowls and pipes with shell inlay attest to the refined skill of Chumash artisans. These beautiful works of art were useful as well.

Chumash basketry was recognized for its outstanding quality and design. The Chumash made two kinds of baskets—coiled and twined. To make a coiled basket, a basket maker wove whole rush stems (branches from a reedy plant that grows in marshy areas) into geometric patterns. A twined basket was made from smaller pieces of rush stems or deer grass. These grass-and-willow baskets were so tightly woven that they could hold water.

(Below) *A Chumash weaver interspersed blades of dyed grass with the natural blades to create the geometric pattern of this basket.* (Bottom) *The Chumash used rush, a strong-bladed grass native to marshy areas, to make baskets.*

(Below) *The Chumash carved mortar holes into the bedrock.*

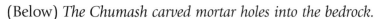

The Chumash built dome-shaped houses that were almost waterproof. Workers first stripped willow poles of their bark. Builders then pounded the poles several inches into the ground in a circle approximately 15 feet wide. The next step was to bend the poles toward the center of the circle and to tie their tops together with rope. Builders layered this frame with tightly woven tule mats. They were careful to leave an opening at the top of the dome-shaped home for the chimney hole and an opening on the side to serve as a door. Inside a dwelling, the family built a fire in the center and placed sleeping mats in a circle around it.

In addition to homes, most Chumash villages also had a ceremonial dance ground, a playing field, the village burial ground, and *temescales*, or

(Above) *This **shaman** (priest), wearing ceremonial clothing and **body paint,** prepares to perform a Chumash ritual.*

(Left) *The Chumash used the morning glory to make a strong, herb-filled drink. In combination with fasting, prayers, and offerings, the drink was believed to ease communication with the supernatural world.* (Above, below, and right) *Examples of the round images that were part of the ritual vision*

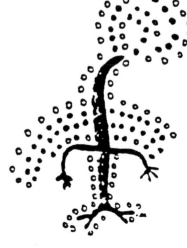

sweatlodges. Chumash men used these buildings—which were dug into the ground and covered with woven tree branches and mud—for purifying rituals before a hunt or before other important events. The men gathered daily in the sweatlodges and sat around a roaring fire. Sometimes they sang songs as they wiped the sweat from their bodies. When they had perspired long enough, the men ran from the temescale and leaped into the nearest body of water to cool off.

The Chumash had a complicated social structure and system of government. A Chumash village was divided first into families and then into classes, **brotherhoods** (craft organizations), and groups of chiefs, doctors, and other ruling persons. Chiefs, called *wots*, governed the village with the help of other officials. A Chumash person's place in the governmental hierarchy was based on family connections and on wealth.

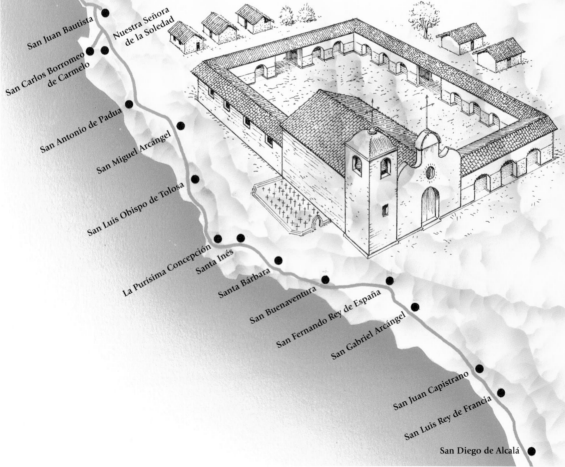

(Above) *This doorway and cloister (covered passage) are part of Mission Santa Bárbara, one of the Spanish missions that had a large population of Chumash.* (Left) *This mission layout was typical of most of the missions in California.*

San Juan Bautista
Nuestra Señora de la Soledad
San Carlos Borromeo de Carmelo
San Antonio de Padua
San Miguel Arcángel
San Luis Obispo de Tolosa
La Purísima Concepción
Santa Inés
Santa Bárbara
San Buenaventura
San Fernando Rey de España
San Gabriel Arcángel
San Juan Capistrano
San Luis Rey de Francia
San Diego de Alcalá

Religion was an important part of Chumash culture. The Chumash believed that supernatural beings, called First People, created the earth. Their world was divided into three layers—the sky, the earth, and the underground. Powerful supernatural beings lived in the middle layer until a great flood covered the land. Then most First People turned into animals, plants, or natural forces such as thunder and lightening. A few First People—including Moon, Morning Star, and Sun and his daughters—went to live in the upper layer, where they became the Sky People. The Chumash believed that one of these Sky People called *Snilemun*, or Coyote of the Sky, created human beings. Humans occupied the middle layer, which a giant eagle separated from the top layer. Dangerous creatures that the Chumash called *nunashish* dwelled in the bottom layer. During the night, nunashish crawled into the middle level and tried to scare or hurt humans.

Religious leaders known as shamans provided a link between humans and the Sky People. Shamans helped villagers interpret dreams, name children, read the stars, predict the weather, and find their **'atishwin** (spirit helper). The 'atishwin guided a person in his or her life decisions. Most important, shamans used herbs and medicines to heal the physical and mental

(Above) *Erosion has severely damaged these rock paintings in the San Egmidio Mountains. They remain the most elaborate rock art in Chumash territory. The usual colors of white, black, red, and yellow dominate, but this ancient artist also used orange, blue, and green to depict variations of the sun and mysterious humanlike beings.* (Right) *A researcher uses a magnifier to study tiny traces of paint on the face of a rock ledge.*

illnesses of the group members. To heal someone, the shaman drank a potion, made from herbs collected in the area, that brought forth visions. Then the shaman used rock paintings to communicate with the spirit world. The act of creating, along with the rites and prayers, caused the symbols to have spiritual and sacred meaning. It's difficult to know for sure, but modern scientists think that the images described the mythic world of the shaman. Shamans may have read the symbols as words of advice from the spirit world.

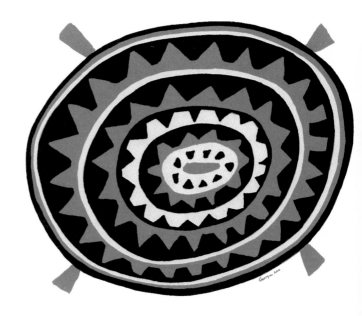

(Below) *The Chumash painted this cave ceiling using natural pigments that they gathered. Ocher (traces of iron ore found in rocks) provided red and yellow pigments, bird droppings or crushed shells made white, and black came from crushed charcoal. Artists sometimes mixed pigments with plant juice or animal fat to make the paint easier to spread.* (Right, top to bottom) *Drawings of circles within circles, as in this painting from Carrizo Plain, are common in Chumash rock art. The Chumash shaman took many forms. The middle figure, from Burro Hats, depicts a shaman while the bottom figure, from Painted Rock, shows a shaman personifying a bear.*

Few material traces of the Chumash remain. There are cave paintings, occasional archaeological discoveries, and some objects on display in museums. Nevertheless, many families claim to be descendants of the Chumash. Most live in the coastal regions of California, either on a small reservation in the town of Santa Inez or in the nearby cities of Santa Barbara and Ventura. But because the languages of the Chumash people have died out, stories of their culture that were passed down from one generation to the next have been lost. In the early twentieth century, John Peabody Harrington, an anthropologist and linguist, spent years interviewing elderly Chumash who still remembered the old customs. His efforts gathered much of what we know about the culture.

The following story is fictional, but the characters and events are based on the information Harrington and others have compiled. Let's travel 500 years back in time to spend a day in a Chumash village. The names of the villagers you'll meet, such as Chulu and Kewen, are real names taken from Harrington's notes.

PART TWO

A DAY WITH CHULU, A CHUMASH CANOE BUILDER

As the sky turns pale just before the sun comes up, Chulu pushes aside the door flap and crawls out of his thatched home. Chulu's dwelling is one of many clustered on high ground overlooking a beach and the Pacific Ocean. As he always does, Chulu begins his day with the steep climb to the *sawi'l*, a small stone shrine that sits on a hill above his village. Dawn is a special and powerful time for the Chumash. As the sun rises over the mountain peaks, Chulu pays homage to the Sky People. He says a prayer and makes an offering of chia seeds and tobacco. Chulu stands facing the sun in the east when his teenage son, Kewen, joins him.

This is a big day for Kewen and his peers, who are called initiates. They'll visit the old shaman Silkiset who lives in the mountains. Silkiset will teach the young people the myths and legends of their tribe and will help them find a spirit helper. Chulu and Kewen face the rising sun together and sing a prayer, asking for the blessing of the sun god.

The two head back home as the village begins to come to life. They pass Chulu's cousins loading their tomol, or canoe, for a day of fishing. The tomol belongs to the family, and Chulu is part of their brotherhood, a group of crafts-people in charge of building and maintaining the village canoes. Normally he would accompany them out to sea, but instead he will lead the group of youngsters on their trek into the mountains.

As they approach the house, Chulu notices a plume of smoke coming from the chimney and knows his wife Melelene is preparing breakfast. Inside, Melelene stirs the fire and pours water from the water bottle, called an *'awaq,* into one of her tightly woven *wakik* (cooking baskets). She is well known in the village for her beautiful baskets, which she learned to make by watching her grand-mother. Melelene's oldest daughter Lekte stirs the *islay,* a meal ground from the seeds of a holly-leafed plant. The meal is mixed with water and boiled over the fire in a stone bowl.

As they cook breakfast, Melelene and Lekte talk. "This will be a busy day, Lekte," Melelene says. "We have a lot to do to prepare for the feast. We have to gather berries and make acorn meal."

Lekte smiles. "Yes, this is a special day for everyone. Kewen will find his dream helper, and tonight they will dance the seaweed dance. I can hardly wait!"

In accordance with tradition, young people on this special occasion fast and pray before visiting the old shaman, so Kewen won't be eating breakfast. For the past 10 days, Kewen has been preparing himself by not eating salt or meat. And everyday he has gone to the temescale to purify his body. If an initiate has not purified himself or herself properly or has violated some **ritualistic law,** then a spirit helper will not appear to that person.

After Chulu has breakfast, he and Kewen walk down to the beach to watch Chulu's cousins launch the canoe. Kewen's favorite uncle, Kwaiyin, greets Kewen. "Today you will see your 'atishwin, Kewen. You must be brave. Perhaps it'll be one of the two most powerful dream helpers, bear or rattlesnake. My dream helper is *helek*, falcon. He warns me of danger." As he spoke, Kwaiyin touched a small stone **effigy** of a falcon he kept in a small bag suspended from his waist.

Chulu and Kewen watched Kwaiyin and the other men wade out into the water and climb into the tomol. Kwaiyin calls, "I hope to catch a tuna for tonight's feast. Good luck, Kewen." He waves at them, and the men paddle off through the surf.

**T**he pair walked farther down the beach to meet several village men who are part of the Brotherhood of the Tomol. They are working on a new canoe. Canoes can take as long as six months to build. A couple of months ago, Chulu helped plane the planks that make up the tomol's sides. The planks had to be split, smoothed with a stone cutting tool called an **adze,** and then sanded with a rough piece of sharkskin. The men then drilled holes in the plank ends and made *miyash* (string) from *tok* (hemp) to tie the boards together. The final steps are to waterproof the canoe with a mixture of pitch and tar called *yop* and then to paint and decorate it.

Kewen helps stir the boiling yop in a large pot carved from a soft stone called steatite. When Kewen notices that the mixture looks runny he asks, "Should I add more tar to the mixture, Father? Shouldn't it be thicker to waterproof the canoe?"

"You're right, Kewen," Chulu agrees. "Go ahead and add some more."

When the tar comes to a boil, one brotherhood member, Ti'mi, begins to apply the sticky black mixture to the edge of a board. Chulu stands back and admires the canoe. "This will be a fine tomol. It will carry us safely to the island villages. How shall we decorate it?"

"Let's paint it with *woqo* (red ocher and pitch) and then put some abalone shell on the prow," Ti'mi replies. Kewen watches closely as his father and Ti'mi decorate the canoe. When Kewen is an adult, he'll become a member of the brotherhood and he will make canoes like his father and uncle.

Kewen's great uncle, Yanonali, is the village *wot*, or chief. He is on his way to the temescale and stops to wish Kewen good luck. "Well Kewen, today is your initiation. I hope that it goes well for you and that you become a fine hunter." Yanonali removes a leather thong from around his neck. An abalone pendant that shimmers in the sunlight hangs from the thin leather band. "This is for you, Kewen. Wear it always, for it has magic powers."

Chulu replies, "Thank you, Yanonali, for the honor you pay to my son."

Turning to Kewen he adds, "It's time to begin the long walk into the hills. Follow me, Kewen. Your uncle, Alow, and three of your cousins are coming along."

Soon, those who are going on the trip arrive at Chulu's home. Kewen greets his cousins and close friends, Mushu and Kipomo. Another cousin, Luhui, joins the group. Kewen is particularly fond of Luhui. She's very pretty with her long black hair shining in the sunlight. The group talks about how nervous they are. They worry that they might not find spirit helpers. Not everyone has such a vision. How would they get through their lives without one? It was a frightening thought.

Chulu senses their nervousness and smiles as he remembers how he felt before his initiation. He knows that they'll be fine. He takes his bow and arrow, and the group begins walking toward the mountains. Chulu and his brother will leave the initiates with the old shaman and then go hunting for deer. The deer meat will be a tasty addition to the feast that will greet the returning initiates.

Once out of the village, the small group walks through the long grass and past a stand of giant oak trees. Beneath the oaks, on a ledge of sandstone, several village women grind acorn flour by pounding acorns in mortars built into the bedrock. They look up and smile when the initiates walk past. "Good luck!" a few of them shout.

As the group walks on, the path grows steeper. They must scramble over rocks and climb ever higher. When a hawk soars overhead, Chulu says, "Look, *helex*, a good sign. The hawk is a messenger." They wade across a sparkling creek to continue their climb up a large sandstone ledge. The stones eventually give way to a grassy meadow.

From this meadow, they can see over the mountains and green valleys all the way to the distant blue sea. The islands where some of Chulu's cousins live are barely visible on the horizon. At the other edge of the meadow is Silkiset's cave.

As the group of initiates enters Silkiset's shaman cave, Kewen marvels at the colorful paintings of circles, shapes, and figures that adorn its walls. The old shaman's long, gray hair contrasts with his feathered headdress. Two necklaces made of bear claws cross his painted chest. He sits, with his dog at his side, behind a row of three small, steatite bowls filled with pigments—red, white, and black. A larger bowl contains a dark liquid. Kewen shudders slightly, and Chulu puts his hand on his son's shoulder to comfort him. In turn, each initiate presents Silkiset with a gift—a string of shell beads, a deer whistle, a leather pouch filled with chia seeds, and, from Luhui, a beautiful little basket.

The initiates sit in a half circle around Silkiset facing the vivid images on the cave wall. The old shaman begins to speak. "The world is made up of three levels. We live in the middle level, where islands are surrounded by the sea. Slo'w, the giant eagle, supports the level above our world, where the powerful First People live. In the land below, two giant serpents hold up the islands and the sea in the land of *nunashish,* or dangerous creatures. Earth is the mother of us all. Sun is the chief god, an old man who runs across the sky with a firebrand in his hand. Sun lives in a crystal house with two daughters who wear aprons made of live rattlesnakes."

Kewen realizes that the shaman has de-scribed the images on the wall. There on the cave wall in bright red, black, and white is the flat, round world, the serpents, and the eagle. Many of the designs are circles within circles.

Silkiset next tells the initiates how people got their hands. "Coyote of the Sky, Sun, Moon, Morning Star, and the Great Eagle argued over whether people should have hands like Coyote. Coyote won the debate and was just about to stamp his hand down on a beautiful smooth white rock (which would have set the pattern of humans forever) when little Lizard reached out and pressed his own handprint on the stone. Coyote was furious but could do nothing. If Lizard had not interfered, humans would have hands like Coyote today." Chulu smiles to himself. He knows all of Coyote's stories, and some are quite funny.

Silkiset continues. "The morning and evening stars are the wives of the sun. The sun rises in the heart of the east, or *Chposh'ulop*. The rainbow is the work of the spirits. White represents wind, red is fire, and blue is rain. The Milky Way is the path taken by souls of the dead."

Then Silkiset begins to sing, "The sun is the beauty of the earth, giving light to the world." The initiates join in singing this ancient, well-known song. Kewen steals a glance at his cousin Luhui. Her dark eyes are glistening and her cheeks are flushed. He wonders if she feels afraid.

Silkiset says, "Three things are important: *muptamai* (memory), *pitahsi* (understanding), and *kipshuwashich* (will power). If you're good, you'll live well. You're grown now and master of your own opinion. I will die soon, but remember that there is a star that looks over the world, and he looks for all."

Sternly he adds, "Never do anything unlawful and think that no one will see you. For while the sun is shining, an eye is upon you. After dark *Hutash* (the evening star) will be watching."

Silkiset begins to chant, "Drink of the sacred herbs that I have gathered with care and then sleep and dream. The spirit helper that will guide you for the rest of your life will appear in your dream. Your spirit helper will give you a song." He paints stripes on their cheeks with red pigment. They drink from the big bowl filled with dark liquid as he continues chanting.

ith the initiation well under way, Chulu and Alow slip away to go hunting. "Let's go over to the meadow in the next valley," Alow says. "I've heard that's a good place to find deer." The two men walk quietly, watching for signs of game. At the edge of the valley, they pause beneath a large tree to tie their stone arrowheads to their arrows. Then they drape their bodies in deerskin, cover the tops of their heads with stuffed deer heads, and tie them around their chins with leather strings. The disguise allows them to sneak up on the deer without frightening them away. The closer they get, the better their chances are. Soon the men see a stag in the meadow. He pricks up his ears as they approach but is fooled by their disguises. Both men shoot their arrows until the deer falls to the ground, dead.

"Well, there's our feast for tonight," says Chulu. They quickly clean the deer and tie its legs to a pole for the trip back to the village. Before leaving, they place a bit of tobacco and a pinch of chia seeds on the spot where the deer died. Chulu says, "Thank you, deer, for providing us with food. May your spirit live forever."

In the old shaman's cave, the young initiates sleep fitfully as Silkiset waits outside. Soon Kewen and his friends begin to wake from their dreams. As they open their eyes, Silkiset asks each one, "What did you see? What did you dream?" When they answer, he asks, "What song did they give you? What did they say to you?"

At first, Kewen is dazed, but then remembers his dream. It was of *hus* (bear), a powerful dream helper. It was so real! Bear had spoken to him, had told him a song, and had promised to protect him forever. One of his cousins had seen *ha'u* (fox), and another rattlesnake. The others saw birds. Luhui had seen *pilipil* (egret), and she was bright with excitement. Pilipil was the 'atishwin of Luhui's grandmother and was the dream helper she had wanted the most.

As the young people follow Silkiset down the path to the village, Chulu walks down the trail to greet them. He is anxious to hear what dream helper his son had seen and to make sure all went well. Chulu is pleased to learn that Kewen saw xus. The powerful dream helper will keep his son safe in his life journey.

**N**ight has fallen by the time the initiates arrive in the village. The scents in the air let them know that the feast is ready. Chulu and Kewen greet their family as musicians play. Whistles and *tiwalu'lay* (flutes fashioned from bone or reed) are accompanied by rattles made of turtle shells and deer hoofs. Chulu reminds Kewen that these sounds are the voices of the gods.

The *paha*, Halashu, is in charge of the feast. At his signal, the seaweed dance begins. Two men and a woman wear feathered headdresses called *tsuh* and feathered skirts. Their graceful motions imitate the movement of seaweed. The last part of the seaweed dance is performed later in the evening, when the constellation of Pleiades shines high in the sky.

The spectators can't see into the **siliyik,** the most sacred part of the ceremonial ground. The siliyik is a hallowed enclosure that represents the center of learning. Only those men who are **'antap,** or part of the elite class of ruling officers, can participate in the rituals that take place there. Sitting with his family, Kewen listens closely to the words of the songs. The initiation rite has made him an adult member of the tribe, so he has responsibilities. The north star, *minimol*, shines brightly as sparks from the fire dance in the darkness.

Kewen hears the words.

Listen! Listen!
In the land where I was born
never does a foreigner dare
to say that this land is his.
We shall endure.

The old shaman steps forward from his place in the circle and speaks to the crowd. "Look! None of us controls our destiny, for we live in the shadow of the sun. Have courage! You who have families, you, fathers of families, be concerned that if you are not sensitive to your household, it will be like the barren fields. The hour arrives when the owl closes her eyes. Be careful of all the dangers. Hutash is the mirror of the sun, and the sun is the mirror of Hutash." He shakes the staff he holds and uses it to pound three times on the ground.

'Alahtin, a full moon, shines brightly. Chulu knows this is a good sign, for the moon has the power to cleanse things. Feather banners stir in the breeze. "It's a good life," Chulu thinks as he says a silent prayer.

AFTERWORD

The words of the song at the end of the story suggest that the Spaniards had arrived in Chumash territory. In 1542 the Spanish explorer Juan Rodríguez Cabrillo sailed northward from the Spanish colony of Mexico along what came to be known as the California coast. When the Chumash saw the European ships approaching, they paddled out to welcome the newcomers and invited them to stay in the village. And when Cabrillo's party left, the Chumash supplied them with food for their journey.

In 1769 the Spaniards returned and claimed present-day California for Spain by establishing missions all along the coast. The purpose of the missions was to convert the Native Americans to Christianity and to teach the Chumash Spanish customs. Although some of the Chumash came to the missions willingly, Spanish missionaries, called padres, lured other Chumash with gifts. After the padres baptized the Native Americans, they forced them to stay in crowded **barracks** on the mission grounds and to work long hours without pay. Many Chumash became ill and died from diseases, such as smallpox, measles, and mumps, carried unknowingly by the Europeans.

By 1821 Mexico had become an independent country with claims to California. The Mexican government **secularized** the missions in 1834. The padres went back to Spain, and settlers from Mexico took control of the mission lands. Although the Chumash were free, many had forgotten or had never been free to learn their traditional lifeways.

The Chumash lost more of their land to white settlers during the California gold rush that began in 1849. By the early 1900s, the Chumash had been driven to near extinction, and only a few Chumash tribal members remained.

In modern times, a few descendants of the Chumash live on the Santa Ynéz Reservation, 75 acres of land set aside for them by the U.S. government in 1901. But most Chumash make their homes in the Santa Barbara area, where they work to preserve their culture.

GLOSSARY

adze: A sharp metal or stone tool used for shaping wooden boards.

animist: A person who believes that objects in nature and acts of nature are filled with spiritual power.

'antap: An elite class of ritual officers who made up a powerful religious group. Members were political and religious leaders who performed dances at ceremonies. The leader of the 'antap was called a *paha*.

'atishwin: A dream or spirit helper who ensured general blessings, good health, and long life. The dream helper offered power and protection and usually appeared in animal form.

barracks: A building or set of sparse buildings used to house soldiers or workers.

body paint: A painted pattern applied to the face and body. Each Chumash village had a distinctive pattern. Special designs were painted for ceremonial dances.

brotherhood: An organization of specialists, based on kinship. Members of the Brotherhood of the Tomol were responsible for caring for a canoe and its possessions. They also operated as sea traders, transporting goods between the mainland and islands or along the coast to other mainland villages.

chia: A protein-rich oily seed from the sage plant that was highly nutritious and used as food.

effigy: A carved stone object that served as a talisman (charm) and often represented the carrier's 'atishwin. The Chumash considered these simple carvings alive and powerful and carried them around as visible spirit helpers. Holding a talisman activated its power and in times of stress provided a sense of well-being and strength. The Chumash carefully guarded their effigies by wrapping them in eagle down or beads and storing them in a small pouch.

obsidian: A smooth black stone created when lava cools.

piñon: The nut of the pine nut tree, used as food.

ritualistic law: A rule or set of rules that members of a society establish and follow to uphold certain religious or social customs.

rock painting: A form of art applied to rocks. To the Chumash, rock painting was linked to communication with the spirit world. The act of creating the art, along with the rites and prayers that accompanied it, gave the symbols spiritual and sacred meaning.

secularize: To transfer from religious to nonreligious use.

shaman: A priest who is highly respected and feared for his supernatural powers. Shamans cured the sick, communicated with the gods, and looked after the psychic well-being of the people.

shell beads: A form of money, decoration, and jewelry. Abalone shells made lustrous pendants; clamshells were used for beads and money. A univalve was a favorite bead material, and keyhole limpets were used as hair ornaments. Shell money had relative values depending upon the type and was traded for obsidian and rare pigments from the Sierra Nevada to the east. The Chumash were among the wealthiest of California Indians, furnishing most of the supply of clamshell money for southern California.

siliyik: A sacred enclosure where ceremonies and rituals took place. Placed within a dancing ground and marked by banners, the siliyik represented the center of learning. The Chumash could not enter the hallowed ground unless they were members of the 'antap.

soapstone: A soft, grayish green or brown stone found on Santa Catalina Island. The Chumash used the stone to create bowls that were carefully polished, engraved with elegant designs, and inlaid with shell beads. Although the Chumash knew about pottery from contact with peoples to the south, they preferred bowls from soapstone because they could be heated directly on the fire without breaking.

tomol: An oceangoing sewn plank canoe, the only one made in the Western Hemisphere. Sometimes as long as 24 feet, tomols were embellished with paint, shell inlay, or both. Tomols made fishing and trading more efficient.

PRONUNCIATION GUIDE

abalone	ah-buh-LOH-nee
'Alahtin	AH-lakh-tihn
'antap	AHN-tahp
'atishwin	AH-tish-wuhn
'awaq	AH-wahk
Chposhʻulop	CHUH-pohsh-oo-lohp
Chumash	CHOO-mahsh
haʻu	HAH-oo
hus	HOOS
kipshuwashich	KIHP-shoo-wah-shuhch
miyash	MEE-yahsh
muptamai	MOOP-tah-my
nunashish	NOO-nah-shuhsh
piñon	PIHN-yohn
pitahsi	PEE-takh-suh
sawiʻl	SHAH-wihl
shaman	SHAH-mehn
siliyik	SEE-lee-yuhk
Snilemun	SHNEE-lay-moon
steatite	STEE-uh-tight
temescale	tay-mehs-KAHL
tiwaluʻlay	TEE-wah-loo-lie

FURTHER READING

Behrens, June. *Missions of the Central Coast.* Minneapolis: Lerner Publications Company, 1996.

Blakely, Martha. *Native Americans and the U.S. Government.* New York: Chelsea Juniors, 1995.

Brown, Fern G. *American Indian Science: A New Look At Old Cultures.* New York: Twenty-First Century Books, 1997.

Edwards, Carolyn McVickar. *Sun Stories: Tales from Around the World to Illuminate the Days and Nights of Our Lives.* New York: HarperCollins, 1995.

Gibson, Robert, O. *The Chumash.* New York: Chelsea House Publishers, 1990.

Jones, Jayne Clark. *The American Indians in America. Vol. II: The Late 18th Century to the Present.* Minneapolis: Lerner Publications Company, 1991.

Liptak, Karen. *North American Indian Ceremonies.* New York: First Book, 1992.

Liptak, Karen. *North American Indian Medicine People.* New York: First Book, 1990.

Margolin, Malcolm and Yolanda Montijo. *Native Ways: California Indian Stories and Memories.* Berkeley, CA: Heyday Books, 1995.

Mayo, Gretchen Will. *Star Tales. North American Indian Stories About the Stars.* New York: Walker Publishing Company, Inc., 1987.

Monroe, Jean Guard and Ray A. Williamson. *First Houses: Native American Homes and Sacred Structures.* Boston: Houghton Mifflin Company, 1993.

Pelta, Kathy. *California.* Minneapolis: Lerner Publications Company, 1995.

INDEX

ABOUT THE
AUTHOR AND THE ILLUSTRATOR

Georgia Lee is an archaeological laureate from the University of California at Los Angeles with a specialization resulting from six years of field study on Easter Island. She is also an advanced primitive art laureate from the University of California at Santa Barbara. She serves as a researcher for the Santa Barbara Museum of Natural History. Near this city, Lee has documented the rock paintings of the Chumash. One of Dr. Lee's fundamental concerns is the conservation of archaeological sites. She lectures annually on this theme and also serves as the national president on the Committee for the Conservation and Preservation of the American Rock Art Research Association.

Giorgio Bacchin, a native of Milan Italy, studied the graphic arts in his hometown. After years of freelance graphic design, Mr. Bacchin has completely devoted himself to book illustration. His works have appeared in educational and trade publications.

an imprint of
■SCHOLASTIC
www.scholastic.com

Scholastic and Tangerine Press and associated logos are trademarks of Scholastic Inc.

Published by Tangerine Press, an imprint of Scholastic Inc., 557 Broadway; New York, NY 10012

10 9 8 7 6 5 4 3 2 1

ISBN-10: 0-545-08504-7
ISBN-13: 978-0-545-08504-5

Printed and bound in China

Scholastic Canada, Ltd.
Markham, Ontario

Scholastic Australia Pty. Ltd
Gosford NSW

Scholastic New Zealand, Ltd.
Greenmount, Auckland

About the Authors

Peter Batson is a New Zealand-based marine scientist and photographer who has participated in many deep-sea expeditions. He is a co-founder of photo agency DeepSeaPhotography.com, and many of his photos appear in this book. He also is a director of DeepOcean Quest Productions.

A trained biologist, Dr. Brian Batson co-manages DeepOcean Quest Productions, a company that focuses on bringing the deep sea to life through film, animation, and educational outreach.

Photo Credits:

P4-5, © DeepSeaPhotography.com; P6-7 Twilight Zone, © DeepSeaPhotography.com; Dark Zone, © Dr. Kevin Raskoff; The Abyss, © Dr. Kevin Raskoff; P8-9 background and pressure © DeepSeaPhotography.com, Jelly, © Dr. Steven Haddock, Anglerfish and Viperfish © ImageQuestMarine.com; P10 © DeepSeaPhotography.com; P11 © Angler fish, © ImageQuestMarine.com; P12 © Dr. Steven Haddock; P13 © ImageQuestMarine.com; P14 © ImageQuestMarine.com; P15 © ImageQuestMarine.com; P16 © ImageQuestMarine.com; P17 © DeepSeaPhotography.com; P18 © DeepSeaPhotography.com; P19 © DeepSeaPhotography.com; P20 © DeepSeaPhotography.com; P21 © DeepSeaPhotography.com; P22 © DeepSeaPhotography.com; P23 © DeepSeaPhotography.com; P24 © Dr. Kevin Raskoff; P25 © Dr. Kevin Raskoff; P26 © Dr. Steven Haddock; P27 © Dr. Steven Haddock; P28 © Dr. Steven Haddock; P29 © DeepSeaPhotography.com; P30-31 © Dr. Kevin Raskoff; P32 © Dr. Steven Haddock, P33 © DeepSeaPhotography.com; P34 © DeepSeaPhotography.com; P35 © DeepSeaPhotography.com; P36 © DeepSeaPhotography.com; P37 © DeepSeaPhotography.com; P38 © DeepSeaPhotography.com; P39 © DeepSeaPhotography.com; P40 © ImageQuestMarine.com; P41 © Dr. Kevin Raskoff; P42 © DeepSeaPhotography.com; P43 © ImageQuestMarine; P44 © DeepSeaPhotography.com; P45 © Dr. Kevin Raskoff; P46 © DeepSeaPhotography.com; P47 © Dr. Steven Haddock

Dedication:

To Jacob Keane

Acknowledgment:

We'd like to thank Dr. Steven Haddock, Dr. Kevin Raskoff, and David Batson (DeepOceanQuestProductions) for their input.